Can you really fry an egg on a stone?

Disney BOOKS BY MAIL

DK Direct Limited
Managing Art Editor Eljay Crompton
Senior Editor Rosemary McCormick
Writer Alexandra Parsons
Illustrators The Alvin White Studios and Richard Manning
Designers Amanda Barlow, Veneta Bullen, Richard Clemson,
Sarah Goodwin, Diane Klein, Sonia Whillock

Contents

How do thermometers work?

At the bottom of the hollow glass tube on a thermometer, there's a bulb full of liquid. Liquid takes up more space as it heats up. The more the temperature rises, the more space the liquid needs, so it has to move up the narrow glass tube.

4

Taking your temperature
Your normal body temperature is 98.6°F. If it goes up, it means you're probably not feeling too well.

Hot and cold facts

☞ Just like people in different places measure distance in either miles or kilometers, temperature is also measured in two different ways. When you see the letter F next to a temperature number, that means Fahrenheit. When you see the letter C next to a temperature number, that means Centigrade.

5

Can you really fry an egg on a stone?

Yes, you can. That's because when stone gets hot, it keeps its heat and eggs will cook at a low temperature. So, if a stone has been in the sun for a long time and you touch it and say –"Ouch!"– it's probably hot enough to cook your eggs over easy!

6

Running on sunshine
Instead of gas, solar cars run on heat from the sun. Panels on the car collect the heat from the sun and turn it into energy which is stored in batteries. The energy in the batteries gets the car moving.

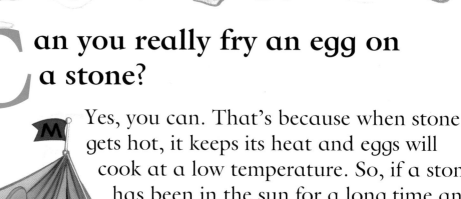

Eggs in a pan
What did the egg say to
the cook?
You crack me up!

Sizzling facts

👉 The sun is so big that you could fit one
million Earths inside of it.

👉 Light from the sun takes around eight
minutes to reach Earth.

👉 The sun is 92,955,900 miles from Earth.
It would take over 200 years to get
there by car.

Is it cold inside an igloo?

No, it's not, it's warm and kind of cozy. The igloo traps air inside it which soon warms up when it's filled with people. Igloos are made from snow that has been hardened by cold winds and frost. Blocks like big bricks are cut out with a special snow knife and then packed closely together.

Hot and cold

A delicious dessert called baked Alaska works the opposite way an igloo does. Meringue (made from egg whites and sugar) on the outside, protects cold ice cream on the inside, so the ice cream doesn't melt, even when you put it in the oven!

Eskimo facts

Eskimos have lived in the Arctic for more than 4,000 years. Some Eskimos still live in igloos, but many now live in houses.

The Eskimos of Greenland and North America are called Inuit. Inuit means "real men."

Why do we keep some foods in the refrigerator?

To keep them from spoiling, or going bad. All fresh foods have bacteria living on them. Bacteria are tiny cells that grow very quickly and make food rot. Storing food in cold places slows down the growth of bacteria and keeps food fresher longer.

Can it!
There are other ways to stop bacteria. Some foods are stored in airtight cans to keep bacteria out. Dried foods, such as raisins, have less water so bacteria can't grow easily.

Food facts

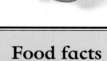 Eskimos keep meat fresh by freezing it in snow.

The first ice cream was made in Ancient Rome, thousands of years ago. It was made from crushed fruit and snow.

How does a thermos work?

It keeps hot things hot and cold things cold because it has two walls – one on the outside and one on the inside. The air in the space between the walls has been pumped out. Because the space is empty, heat and cold can't pass through it. The airless space is called a vacuum.

Don't forget your hat!

If you wear a woolly hat, you stay warm because it keeps your body heat in. People keep houses warm in the same way. They put a special material in their roof to stop warm air from getting out.

12

Thermal facts

☞ Adelie penguins stay warm because they have an outer layer of oily waterproof feathers, an inner layer of fluffy down feathers, AND a layer of fatty blubber.

☞ Thermal underwear keeps us toasty because it traps a layer of warm air next to the skin.

13

What is an iceberg?

Icebergs are large chunks of ice that have broken off the huge icy crusts that cover the coldest parts of the world, like the north and south poles. The largest icebergs are found in the Antarctic Ocean, near the south pole.

Home sweet home

Icebergs are SO big that flocks of penguins live on them. Penguins can't fly, so they waddle along on the ice or, if they're in a hurry, they fall forward onto their chests and slide. Yippee!

Why does ice float?

Because when water freezes it turns to ice, and ice is lighter than water. That's why it floats in the water like a boat!

Brrrrrrrrrrrrr!
Why can't you keep a secret at the north pole? **Because your mouth can't stop chattering!**

Icy facts

☞ When you look at an iceberg, you're only seeing a small part of it. That's because most of it is floating under the water.

☞ Icebergs can move up to 10 miles a day.

☞ Scientists watch icebergs so they can warn ships when icebergs get too close.

Why do we get sunburned?

After we've been in the sun for a while, the sun's rays begin to harm our skin. Skin cells are injured and become painful. And the blood vessels underneath our skin get bigger and allow more blood to flow through. That extra blood is what makes us look sunburned.

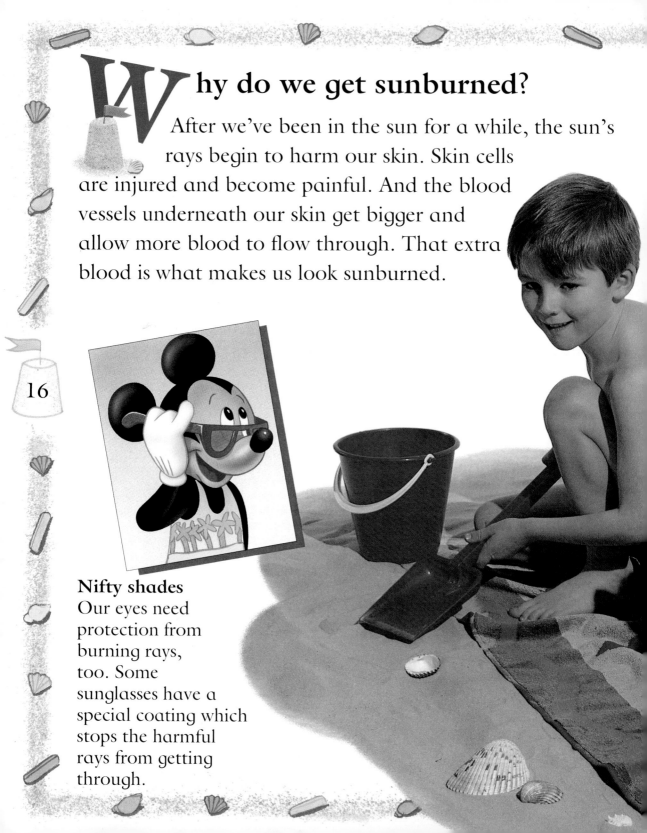

Nifty shades
Our eyes need protection from burning rays, too. Some sunglasses have a special coating which stops the harmful rays from getting through.

Sunny facts

👉 You can get a suntan, even a sunburn, on a cloudy day because burning rays can get through clouds.

👉 Long ago, Eskimos from the Arctic and Maoris from New Zealand thought that the sun took a boat trip every night.

Slap on that lotion!

Sunscreens help block out the sun's burning rays. They have SPF (Sun Protection Factor) numbers. SPF 3 means that you can stay in the sun three times as long as you could without sunscreen and still not burn. SPF 15 means you can stay 15 times longer.

17

Why are some colors cooler than others?

Because more of the sun's warming rays bounce off light colored surfaces than dark colored surfaces. So when you wear colors such as white, light yellow, or light pink you stay a little bit cooler than you would if you wore dark colors.

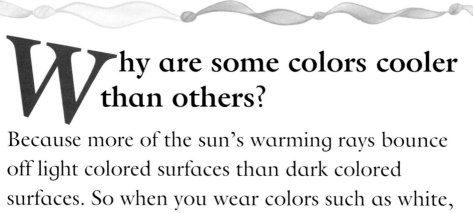

Keep those heat waves out of here!

In hot countries people often paint their houses white on the outside to keep them cooler on the inside.

Hit me with those heat waves!

Dark colors do the opposite of light colors – they soak up heat. That's why gardeners sometimes put black plastic bags around little seedlings to warm them up and help them grow.

Colorful facts

 In some countries red is a sign of danger, but in China, red is the color of happiness.

 In America, the Pueblo Indians have colors, instead of letters, to show directions on a compass. East is white, north is yellow, west is blue, and south is red.

Why do we rub our skin when we're cold?

Because when two things rub against one another, it makes friction – and friction usually makes things hot. So when you rub your skin you are making heat.

Slipping and sliding

Friction not only creates heat, it also helps stop things from slipping. The rougher things are, the more friction there is when they rub together.

Things that are smooth or wet are slippery because they give less friction. That's why you're likely to slip when walking on ice in shoes that are smooth on the bottom.

Friction facts

☞ If you rub two sticks together for long enough, the wood will get so hot it will start a fire.

☞ Brakes on a bicycle use friction to slow the wheels down.

Ice skating
When ice skaters want to stop, they push the jagged part of their skate blade into the ice, which creates friction.

Why does the bathroom mirror steam up?

When you take a shower, it makes the air in the bathroom steamy. Steam is made of tiny droplets of water floating in the air. When the warm, wet air meets a cool surface like a mirror, it turns back into water. Then you get a steamy glass to draw on.

Blowing steam
You can see your breath in winter for the same reason. Warm, moist air from your mouth meets cold air and makes steam.

Where does dew come from?
Dew is moisture from the air that settles on cold surfaces, like leaves, and turns into dew drops during the night.

Misty facts

☞ If you go outside on a misty or foggy day, you are stepping inside a cloud! Fog and mist are really clouds that are close to the ground.

☞ When there's a lot of moisture in the air, it's more difficult to see into the distance.

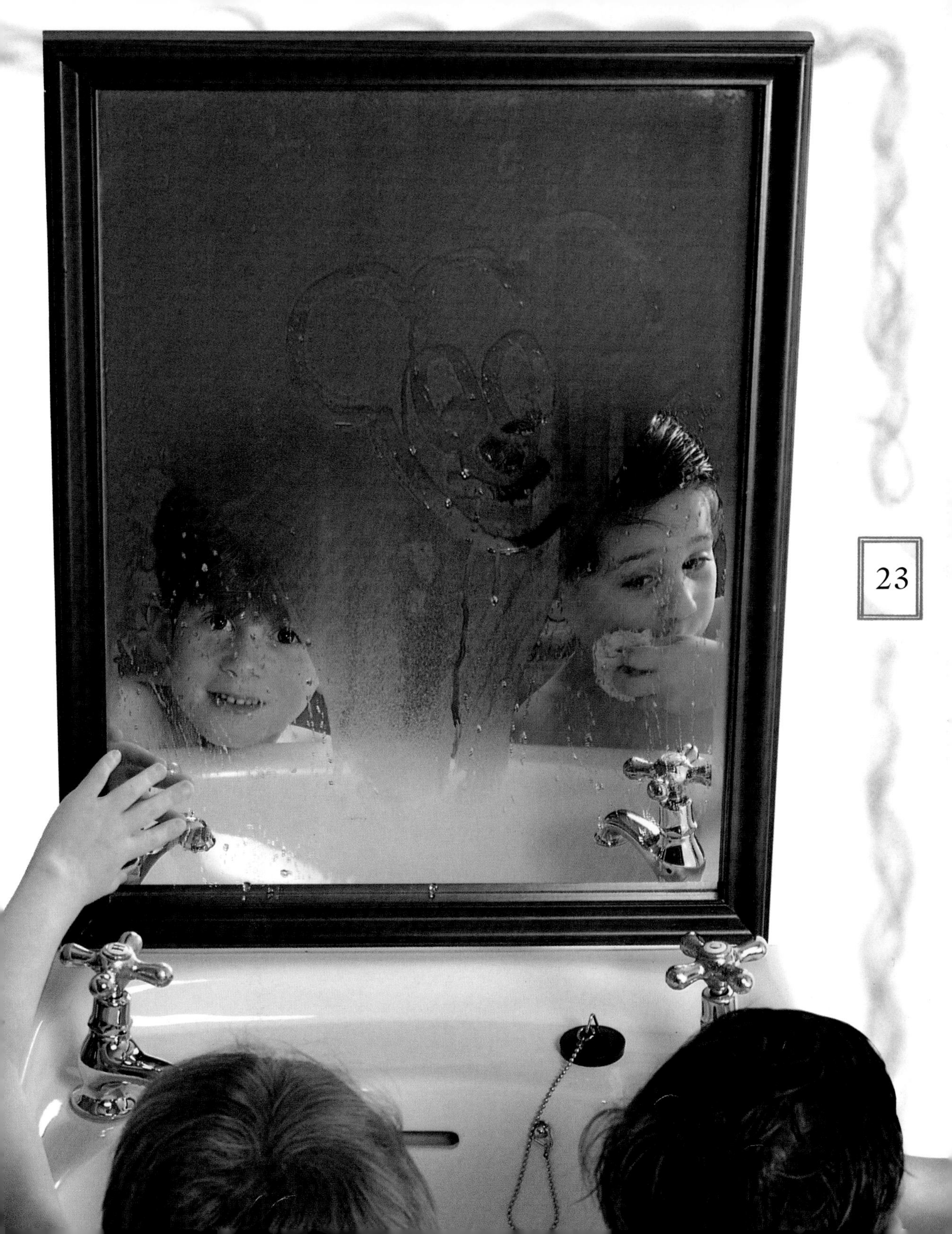

Why do sheep have woolly coats?

To keep them warm when it's cold.

Sheep spend most of the time outdoors, even when it's snowy, so they need a thick coat of wool. This wool coat is called a fleece. When the warm weather comes, farmers clip off the fleece, but the sheep grow a new coat in time for winter.

Snip, snip
This sheep has had half a haircut. Now you can see just how thick that woolly coat is.

Lots of wool

We use sheeps' wool to make clothes. We can also get wool from goats, rabbits, and camels.

Close shave

Shearers use electric shaving combs when they cut off the sheep's wool. It doesn't hurt the sheep one bit!

Woolly facts

☞ The fastest sheep shearers in the world can trim a whole sheep in less than a minute.

☞ In Australia, scientists have made a sheepshearing robot. It's not as quick as a human – but it can work much longer hours!

Woolly gags
"Doctor, doctor, I've just swallowed a sheep."
"How do you feel?"
"Very ba-a-a-ad!"

Why do dogs pant when it's hot?

To cool down. People can cool off by sweating. As sweat dries up it takes heat away with it. But dogs have very few sweat glands, so they have to lose heat by drying up the water on their tongues. That's why they hold their mouths open and stick their tongues out.

Big ears
Desert rabbits lose body heat through their big ears. As blood flows through veins close to the skin in their ears, the blood releases its heat into the air.

Cool kangaroo!

How do kangaroos stay cool? They lick their arms. As their arms dry they cool down.

Chill out!

☞ Reptiles must be in a hot place when they digest their food. If not, the food in their stomach may become so cold that it will lower their body temperature enough to kill them.

☞ Some birds just leave home when it gets too hot. They go somewhere cooler for the summer.

27

Richard and Diane are going on vacation.
Diane is going to chilly Alaska.
Richard is going to sunny Mexico.
Can you help each one decide what to pack?